Original title:
Tropical Lullaby

Copyright © 2025 Creative Arts Management OÜ
All rights reserved.

Author: Levi Montgomery
ISBN HARDBACK: 978-1-80581-601-0
ISBN PAPERBACK: 978-1-80581-128-2
ISBN EBOOK: 978-1-80581-601-0

The Sweetness of Still Waters

In the sun, the palms do sway,
Frogs in hats, they come to play.
Dancing crabs and silly bees,
Sipping nectar, if you please.

A fish in shades, he takes a leap,
While lazy turtles nearly sleep.
The parrots chuckle, oh so loud,
As they parade, oh what a crowd!

Bamboo sticks that tap a beat,
Tickle toes and wiggly feet.
The breeze, it laughs, a gentle tease,
As lizards break into a freeze.

Under stars, the night ignites,
Fireflies having silly fights.
With coconut smiles, we sit so still,
In this sweet place, time bends at will.

In the Shade of Palm Trees

Under palms swaying lightly,
Monkeys swing with great delight.
Coconuts drop with a thud,
Each one's a game of 'who's next bud?'

Seagulls squawk from above,
Chasing dreams of fish love.
Crabs dance in their sideways style,
Pinching toes, now that's worthwhile!

Night Songs by the Sea

The moon whispers silly tales,
Of fish who wear tiny scales.
Stars waltz in a sparkly way,
While crabs rehearse their cabaret.

Shells chuckle in twilight's glow,
As waves perform a crazy show.
Sea cucumbers play the part,
Of underwater work of art!

Butterfly Kisses at Dusk

Butterflies flutter, tickling my nose,
While fireflies twinkle like little prose.
The garden giggles, all in bloom,
As frogs croak their tunes; they'd love a room!

Crickets chirp in offbeat time,
Planning their next big slime climb.
A snail yells, 'I'm winning the race!'
But slow and steady is just his pace!

Sun-Kissed Serenities

Sunshine splashes on the shore,
While dolphins jump and roar.
Sandcastles boast of their height,
Until a wave says, 'Not tonight!'

Sandy toes and laughter loud,
Seashells cheer, they're ever proud.
A crab holds court, quite the fuss,
Declaring himself king—oh, what a plus!

Waves Whispering the Night's Secrets

The waves talk softly, a cheeky chat,
To seashells and fish, under the moon's hat.
They giggle and splash, with a wink of a tide,
Tickling the sand as they rush to hide.

Crabs join the fun, cranking up their dance,
With sideways shuffles, they take a chance.
They jive with the breeze, an odd little crew,
While starfish keep watch, not knowing what to do.

Cotton Candy Skies at Dusk

The sun dips low, in a sugar-glazed hue,
Clouds puff like candy, all pink and askew.
Seagulls are cackling, they squawk with delight,
As the breeze sways trees in a comical plight.

A parrot nearby, with a hat that's too big,
Sips on a coconut, looking quite the fig.
He tells silly tales of a caper or two,
While the ocean waves giggle, just waiting for dew.

The Lull of the Lush Wilderness

In the jungle where critters play peek-a-boo,
Monkeys swing high with their laughable crew.
Sloths hang around, quite the slow-motion show,
While toucans squawk jokes, their beaks in a row.

The leaves start to dance in a cheeky parade,
As frogs croak their tunes, none are ever afraid.
The fireflies blink, with a flicker of glee,
This wild, wondrous world hacks a giggle at me.

Dreams Cast by the Rising Tide

The tide creeps in with a mischievous wink,
Carrying dreams on a foamy little link.
A hermit crab hosts, with a shell as his throne,
Welcoming dreams that feel right at home.

Stars cast their nets, in a twinkling charade,
Catching bright wishes that the tides have made.
Dolphins play tag, with a splash and a flip,
As the moon laughs out loud, on a joy-filled trip.

The Light of Longing Skies

Beneath the moon's silly grin,
Crabs waltz by with a spin.
The parrot laughs at the breeze,
Whispering secrets from the trees.

Stars twinkle like mischief-makers,
Fish tease the lazy snake-ers.
Coconuts giggle, rolling free,
In this night of jubilee.

Echoes of Island Twilight

The sun dips down, a sleepy face,
While turtles race in a slow-paced chase.
Bananas slide in a funny dance,
As shadows stretch for a moonlit prance.

Palm trees sway in a ticklish breeze,
Giggling softly, like best friends, please.
Fireflies flicker with sparkly glee,
Guiding the night, like a party spree.

Dance of the Swaying Sea

Waves chuckle as they tickle the shore,
Shells join in, calling out for more.
Dolphins leap in a joyful spree,
Splashing laughter that's wild and free.

A crab dons shades, looking quite cool,
While the fish gossip, swimming in school.
Every splash is a joke, every wave a cheer,
In the sea's lively world, we have no fear.

Lull of the Melodic Night

In the dark, frogs croak a tune,
Creating beats in the light of the moon.
Chirps and chuckles fill the air,
Rhythms bouncing without a care.

Giggling waves and breezy sighs,
As sleepy stars blink their eyes.
Dreams dance lightly on the breeze,
In this symphony that never flees.

Hummingbird's Whisper

A hummingbird flits by, oh so fast,
With a tiny hat and boots made of glass.
It sips on nectar, a sweet little treat,
Dancing in circles on delicate feet.

It burps with a giggle, a bubbly surprise,
While buzzing and zipping 'neath sunny blue skies.
Friends scatter laughter, oh what a sight,
As the hummingbird twirls in sheer delight.

Stars Over Ocean Waves

Stars twinkle like fish in the night-time sea,
Whispering secrets, come dance with me!
The ocean waves chuckle, rolling in glee,
Tickling the sand as the moon takes a peek.

A crab puts on shades, he's the star of the tide,
Waving his claws, with such silly pride.
The fish all applaud, what a show they create,
In the shimmer and sparkle, they celebrate fate!

Gentle Breezes and Island Dreams

The breeze tells jokes as it swirls through the palm,
Whispering tales that are silly and calm.
It tickles the coconuts, making them sway,
While seagulls chuckle and play hide and pay.

The waves tease the shore, 'Come out for a run!'
So sandcastles tumble, oh what a fun!
Shells giggle together, whispering delight,
As the sun sinks low, painting all in light.

The Song of Distant Shores

From faraway lands, the shores sing a tune,
With ukuleles strumming beneath the bright moon.
A parrot croons loudly, trying to impress,
While crabs do the limbo in sparkly dress.

Fish leap for joy with a splash and a wink,
While the seaweed sways, does it dance or think?
The rhythm of laughter fills up the air,
As all nature giggles, without a care.

A Meadow of Lost Dreams

In a field where hopes reside,
Grazing cows with joyous pride.
They munch on wishes, oh so sweet,
Dreams of dancing on their feet.

Butterflies wear silly hats,
Chasing bees and playful cats.
Tickling daisies in their play,
Giggles bloom in bright array.

The Sighing Sea

The ocean laughs with salty breeze,
Waves whisper secrets through the trees.
Seagulls sing in tones of jest,
Crabs perform their goofy best.

Fish parade in silly dance,
Jellyfish put on a trance.
Splashing water in delight,
The sea's a stage, so full of light.

Chasing Firefly Dreams

Fireflies twinkle like small stars,
Racing 'round in tiny cars.
They giggle softly as they glow,
Bringing laughter on the go.

In jarred homes, they tell their tales,
Of moonlit nights and wind-swept gales.
With lanterns bright, they light the way,
Making shadows dance and sway.

Under the Canopy of Stars

Beneath a quilt of scattered light,
Silly dreams take off in flight.
Owls wear glasses, looking wise,
As crickets play their lullabies.

Napping frogs in funny hats,
Turn their croaks to random chats.
The night giggles, soft and wide,
As stars wink down, all around.

Midnight in Paradise

Coconuts fall with a whack,
And the parrots squawk and hack.
I scoot away from the beach,
To avoid the crab's sharp speech.

The waves giggle in a swirl,
While the seashells begin to twirl.
A pineapple dreams in the sand,
And offers me a sweet hand.

Mermaids dance with a pot of glue,
While jellyfish shout, "Who are you?"
The palm trees jive with delight,
In the warm glow of the night.

Sandcastles wobble and shake,
As the moon laughs with a quake.
Under the stars, we all prance,
In this absurd, joyous dance.

Coral Reef Reverie

Fish in tuxedos swim around,
As the clams make a clatter sound.
A starfish winks with a sly grin,
While seahorses aim to win.

The seaweed tickles my toe,
And the shells flash their vibrant glow.
A crab conducts the fishy band,
While dolphins leap in stylish strands.

Coral castles rise and sway,
As the turtles groove and play.
An octopus holds a dance-off,
While the clams and mussels scoff.

The sea foam bubbles with cheer,
As the squid shed a happy tear.
In this reef, we all belong,
Singing together our silly song.

Swaying Under the Stars

A coconut juggles with glee,
While the ants dance on the tree.
The breeze tickles the leaves so sweet,
As the crickets tap their tiny feet.

Stars twinkle in a dizzy dance,
A gecko gives a cheeky glance.
The moon grins down at our folly,
While the night wraps us in a jolly.

Bamboo flutes play a funny tune,
As fireflies glow, a natural boon.
Laughter echoes from branch to leaf,
In this lively, blissful reef.

With each sway and with each twist,
Our playful shenanigans persist.
We laugh and twirl, oh what a sight,
Dancing under starlit light.

Starlit Beach Compositions

Sandy toes and silly hats,
Write symphonies with playful spats.
Jellybeans tumble like waves,
As our beach rock band misbehaves.

Everyone joins with a cheer,
With coconuts clinking like beer.
The seagulls join in the fun,
Singing sweet tunes under the sun.

A conch shell blares a wild note,
While the waves steal a giggling boat.
Sand dollars hum a soft beat,
As we shuffle our happy feet.

Under the stars, so divinely,
We compose our songs, oh so whimsically.
With laughter echoing through the night,
Making music, oh what a sight!

Rain Drops on Banana Leaves

Raindrops dance on leaves so green,
They twirl and spin, a funny scene.
Bananas giggle in the breeze,
Swaying softly like they're pleased.

A frog in rubber boots jumps high,
Splashing water as he flutters by.
He tells the flowers a silly joke,
While laughing loudly, not a croak.

The sun peeks out, a cheeky grin,
A party's starting, let's begin!
With hummingbirds in tiny hats,
Sipping nectar, sharing chats.

When evening falls, the fun won't end,
Bouncing on bongo, all are friends.
A fruit parade, oh what a sight,
Banana parties last all night!

The Warmth of Moonlit Waters

The moon's a silver pancake tossed,
In waters warm, at what a cost!
Fish giggle, bumping off the rocks,
Dancing swiftly, wearing socks.

A crab with shades struts on the shore,
Jiving to a rhythm, wanting more.
Stars chuckle softly, casting light,
While jellyfish join the delight.

A dolphin sings a song so bright,
Echoing through the balmy night.
He's off-key but full of glee,
The ocean's chorus sets him free.

With every splash, the fun abounds,
Under the moon, where laughter sounds.
Friends unite on this joyous stage,
Creating waves, at every age!

Star-Kissed Island Nights

Island nights, so bright and bold,
With starry tales that never get old.
A parrot that cracks puns galore,
Sipping punch, always wanting more.

Sea turtles wearing tiny ties,
Chomping seaweed, oh what a prize!
Their slow dance brings a coastal cheer,
While crickets serenade the sphere.

A palm tree sways with a smile so sly,
Dropping coconuts like they're shy.
The beach brigade, with laughter loud,
Join in the fun, a merry crowd.

When dreams take flight, a gentle breeze,
Carrying laughter from the trees.
Under the starlight, life's a game,
Where every night feels just the same!

Calm Currents of the Heart

In gentle waves, the secrets glide,
Whispering tales where laughs reside.
A fish in glasses reading books,
While jellybeans play hide-and-seek in nooks.

The river chuckles, smooth and round,
Creating ripples, a silly sound.
Among the reeds, a turtle teases,
Sharing stories that'll leave you wheezing.

Shells gather close, like friends at play,
Sipping sunshine throughout the day.
With every bubble, silly thoughts fly,
As laughter rises, like clouds in the sky.

From calm to laughter, the heart does sway,
Bubbling freely, come what may.
In the currents of joy, we find our start,
With every wave, we dance, heart to heart.

Coconut Moonbeams

Coconut trees sway with delight,
While monkeys giggle in the night.
Palms rustle secrets under the stars,
As we dance with imaginary cars.

The moon spills laughter on sandy shores,
Crabs are tap dancing; who knows what's in stores?
Brightly colored drinks with tiny umbrellas,
As we toast our joy like silly fella's.

Fireworks of fruit sprout in the sky,
Pineapple hats worn by passersby.
The waves keep rhythm, a joyful beat,
While my coconut buddy does a silly feat.

Giggles echo where sea meets land,
As clowns in coconut shells take a stand.
We leap and twirl in the carefree breeze,
With moonbeam giggles and coconut tease.

Echoes of the Ocean's Breath

Waves are chuckling, what a surprise,
As a fish jumps up, wearing blue ties.
Seagulls squawk jokes from high above,
While dolphins dance in their finned love.

The ocean whispers, 'Don't take it too fast,'
As crabs hold a meeting—what a blast!
Jellyfish giggle in their gooey attire,
While starfish play piano, strumming the wire.

A beach ball bounces, it's off to the moon,
With flip-flops squeaking a jazzy tune.
Sandcastles grinning, wearing silly hats,
While octopuses break dance like acrobats.

With laughter floating on the salty tide,
We chase snails as they try to hide.
Under the sun, with joy in each breath,
The ocean's humor is life's sweetest depth.

Calypso Nightfall

Nightfall dances with a crazy grin,
As fireflies wink, inviting us in.
A parrot squawks a tune from the tree,
While everyone shakes it like they're carefree.

Drums beat loudly, shaking the sand,
While iguanas join a conga band.
The moon peeks down like a curious cat,
To join in the fun and see where we're at.

Bamboo flutes whistle a nonsensical song,
As crickets come hopping along.
In this playful realm, we find our groove,
Under the stars, let's get in the move.

So grab your partner, do the limbo slide,
With giggles and joy as our guide.
Calypso night, you're a party wheel,
As we swirl and twirl, what a fun appeal!

Fireflies and Coconuts

Fireflies flicker like tiny lights,
In the coconut grove, we forget our plights.
With each little blink, they tell us tales,
Of pirate ships sailing and friendly whales.

A monkey swings by, wearing a hat,
Chasing his dreams and an oversized bat.
The coconuts sway, full of sweet cheer,
With giggles and laughter, they draw us near.

The night is alive with a funny crew,
As toucans gossip about what's true.
And the waves roll in, bringing breezy delight,
As we dance with shadows under the night.

Let's chase the fireflies, make wishes come true,
With a coconut drink and a sky so blue.
In this whimsical world where giggles abound,
Let's make this night the quirkiest found.

Tropical Twilight Whispers

In the shade where coconuts sway,
Monkeys dance in a wild ballet.
The parrot squawks a silly tune,
While crabs enjoy a sandy moon.

Laughter spills like a pouring drink,
A turtle winks, what do you think?
The sun dips low, a golden tease,
While fish play tag beneath the trees.

Breezes tickle the palm fronds bright,
As fireflies twinkle, a funny sight.
The night giggles, the stars all grin,
Join the party, let the fun begin!

In the end, it's a raucous cheer,
With creatures sipping on fruity beer.
Tropical fun, a memory to keep,
As we drift off to dream in sleep.

Waves of Surrender

The ocean dances with a splashy leap,
While crabs and fish in a game of keep.
A dolphin jumps, a rascal at heart,
Trying to sell sand, that slippery art!

Seashells whisper their secrets deep,
A seagull swipes a snack, oh what a creep!
While clowns in boats sing silly songs,
The waves giggle, where everyone belongs.

Sunset paints with a brush so bold,
Underneath it, fish tales unfold.
With every wave, the giggles abound,
As the ocean wraps us all around.

At last we sway, on the sandy shore,
Humming along, asking for more.
Under the stars, all worries flee,
We're wrapped in smiles, wild and free.

A Festival of Stars

Beneath the sky where the comets prance,
A party erupts, oh what a chance!
Stars wear hats, each twinkle a flare,
As the moon DJ spins, with style and flair.

The crickets chirp a catchy beat,
While fireflies compete with their glowing heat.
A raccoon joins, with a goofy grin,
Win or lose, it's all in the spin!

Palm trees sway like they're on a glide,
In this festival where joy can't hide.
Balloons drift high, crafted from dreams,
As laughter bubbles, bursting at the seams.

When morning comes, we'll still be here,
Eager to sip on leftover cheer.
With sleepy eyes and hearts so bright,
Every starlit moment feels just right.

Luminous Lagoon Lullabies

In the lagoon where the water glows,
The frogs throw parties, as everyone knows.
Lily pads dance, a concert supreme,
While fishes jump, fulfilling the meme.

The whispers of waves fashion silly tales,
Of mermaids giggling and their flapping scales.
A crab with a top hat struts with glee,
Inviting all to join in jubilee.

Beneath the stars, the glowworms sway,
As the moon beams down, lighting the way.
Every splash is a laugh, every ripple a cheer,
In the luminous lagoon, all are welcome here.

So close your eyes, let the night be wild,
Embrace the fun, like a happy child.
Under the twinkles, sleep will arrive,
In this joyous lagoon, we all come alive.

Dusk's Gentle Embrace

As the sun begins to snooze,
Chickens play in their little shoes.
Mangoes dance with the breeze,
While crabs shuffle with such ease.

The stars peek out for a laugh,
A turtle's trying to take a bath.
Monkeys swing, do the cha-cha,
While parrots squawk, "Hey, buona sera!"

The waves giggle at the shore,
Where sandals float, and dreams restore.
A hammock's strung up in a tree,
Swaying softly, just for me.

With coconut drinks served in style,
Creepy-crawlies break into a smile.
Dusk's embrace brings a parade,
In this fun-filled, twilight escapade.

Rhythms of the Tropics

Dancing leaves in a sunlit breeze,
Rhythmic waves kiss the sand with ease.
A crab with rhythm, moving in line,
Wobbling 'round like a star divine.

The parakeets sing in silly key,
While the sun sets down like a bumblebee.
A monkey juggles coconuts bright,
While lizards wiggle, oh what a sight!

Conga conch shells echo their tune,
Under the watch of a sleepy moon.
The sea cows float, they're in a funk,
Bouncy and jolly, just like a trunk.

All around, the feathers twirl,
As dolphins show off with a swirl.
In this land, where laughter flows,
Nature dances, as daylight slows.

The Dreaming Shore

On the shore where dreams unfold,
Footprints lead to tales retold.
Where seaweed giggles like a friend,
And sandy castles never end.

A seagull steals a chip from a boy,
The laughter cracks like a joyous toy.
Shells whisper secrets to the night,
As fireflies join in the delight.

Waves crash and splash like playful pups,
Tiny fish jump with joyful ups.
Alligators grin, just a bit shy,
While sun tans souls under the sky.

Drifting on a breeze so sweet,
Bananas dance on two left feet.
By this shore, where giggles soar,
Memories linger, forevermore.

Secret Cove Songs

In a cove where secrets dare,
Mermaids giggle in flowing hair.
Dolphins leap with a joyful spin,
As clams start throwing a big shell win.

The tall palm trees sway and sway,
Keeping tune to the night's ballet.
A clam with a crown sings a song,
While fish tap dance all night long.

Coconuts fall, a drumroll here,
As crabs perform without any fear.
The wind flirts with the ocean's song,
Encouraging all to dance along.

In this hidden nook, smiles are free,
Life's a party, just wait and see.
Under stars where mischief flows,
The secret cove, where laughter grows.

Gentle Rhythms of the Ocean

Waves whisper secrets to the shore,
Crabs dance a jig and beg for more.
Seagulls squawk like they own the day,
Shells scatter laughs as they toss and play.

The sun winks down with a golden grin,
While fish swim by in a playful spin.
Bananas float by in a silly parade,
Tropical breezes make shadows cascade.

Harmonies of the Island Heart

Coconuts chuckle on palm tree tops,
While monkeys swing and do funny hops.
The ukulele strums a jolly tune,
As crickets join in, under the moon.

The wind tells tales of a pirate's fate,
While fish wear hats, oh isn't that great?
Island drums beat a jolly refrain,
And laughter bubbles like water from rain.

Swaying to the Calypso Beat

Limbo sticks sway, oh what a sight,
As pineapples dance under the moonlight.
Hula hoops twirl and don't make a fuss,
While turtles groove on the beach like us.

The night air hums with a joyous cheer,
As fireflies twinkle, drawing us near.
Grass skirts twirl with the rhythm so sweet,
Come join the fun, feel the vibrant beat!

Echoes of the Warm Sea Embrace

Starfish gather for a friendly chat,
While sea cucumbers slip and pat.
The ocean giggles with a foamy tide,
As starry nights in the sand abide.

Bamboo flutes play a silly sound,
While jellyfish make blobs all around.
With each gentle wave, laughter does swell,
In this joyous paradise, all is well.

Sand Between Our Toes

We waddle along the shore,
Feet squishy, can't take more.
Seagulls laugh, they caw and dive,
In our flip-flops, we arrive.

Sun tan lotion, quite the smell,
Rub it in, oh what the hell!
Sandy snacks and drinks galore,
Oops, spilled juice; watch it pour!

Our laughter echoes in the breeze,
Tickled toes, and tiny seas.
Crabs are dancing, what a sight,
Under stars, we giggle all night.

With every splash, the world seems bright,
Underneath the glowing moonlight.
We'll cherish these days of fun,
Under the tropical sun!

Silent Night in the Tropics

The moon is high, a silver disk,
Treetops sway, oh, what a whisk!
Chirping frogs sing lullabies,
As fireflies dance in the skies.

Coconuts drop with thuds and bumps,
A sloth's giggle, oh how it jumps!
Palm trees sway in gentle zest,
We lie and dream, this is the best.

A raccoon tries to steal our snack,
With a sneaky step, he's on track.
We throw some grapes, he takes the bait,
Now he's dancing; oh, just wait!

With every chuckle, night unfolds,
In this harmony, life's retold.
Silent night? Oh, that's a joke,
In this paradise, laughter's the smoke!

A Driftwood Dreamscape

Driftwood castles formed with glee,
Flotsam fun for all to see.
Seashells polished by the tide,
In our kingdom, we abide.

A crab parade, oh what a show,
With tiny hats, they steal the glow.
Our laughter echoes on the shore,
Building dreams, we can't ignore.

Soft whispers of the ocean breeze,
Brought our hearts to joyful ease.
Waves tickle toes, what a thrill,
Dance like fish, oh what a skill!

As the sunsets paint the skies,
We gather 'round for one last sigh.
Driftwood dreams and silly schemes,
Carry us to perfect dreams!

The Rhythm of Rainforest

In the jungle, beats arise,
Drip-drop songs that mesmerize.
A parrot's squawk, a monkey's chime,
Nature's giggle, oh, so prime!

Puddles splash where raindrops play,
Hippos dance in a merry display.
With leaves as hats, we spin around,
In this laughter, joy is found.

Frogs in tuxedos croak in style,
While a sloth struts with a grin and guile.
Every rustle, every cheer,
The rainforest calls, come gather near!

With each rhythm, we sway and glide,
Nature's laughter, can't hide, can't hide!
In the heart of this vibrant scene,
Goodbye troubles, hello dream!

Lapping Waves at Dusk

The waves giggle softly, they tease the shore,
With sandcastles crumbling, oh, never a bore.
Crabs dance on their pincers, they put on a show,
As the sun dips down low, putting on a glow.

Flip-flops are flying, oh what a sight!
As people slip, slide, in the fading light.
Seagulls are laughing, they dive for the fries,
Twirling through twilight, like they're in the skies.

Lullabies of the Banyan

The roots are all tangled, a merry old mess,
Monkeys play hide-and-seek, who can guess?
One swings on a branch, then makes a grand leap,
While another just snores, in the shade fast asleep.

Banyan leaves whisper, with secrets they share,
As the sun climbs down, with its golden glare.
Lizards do yoga, a laid-back brigade,
In this leafy realm, where all plans just fade.

Coral Petals and Seafoam

The beach is a canvas, with shells on display,
While starfish are practicing their parade.
Crabs in bow ties, they march with a cheer,
In this underwater gala, we all want to steer.

The waves clap their hands, what a joyful sound!
As colorful fish swim, twirling round and round.
A clam serenades, in a high-pitched tune,
While dolphins are dancing, beneath the big moon.

Parrots in the Twilight

Parrots on branches sing songs of delight,
With voices like trumpets, they pierce through the night.
They gossip and squawk, in vibrant array,
As the world starts to wind down, and children still play.

Their feathers are regal, in colors so bright,
With each playful cackle, they lift up the night.
They sip from their cups, oh what a chime,
As they share tales of mischief, spent in their prime.

Nightfall in the Canopy

The monkeys play tag in the trees,
Swinging and laughing, what a breeze!
An owl hoots loud, trying to be cool,
While frogs croak tunes by the little pool.

A parrot jokes with a silly grin,
Swaying his tail, let the fun begin!
The fireflies dance in a twinkling spree,
Creating a light show just for me!

The palm fronds rustle, a cozy embrace,
Is it a breeze or a tickling face?
Laughter echoed through the warm night,
In this green home, everything feels right.

Under a canopy, stars play peek-a-boo,
While crickets join in with their own tune too.
Nature's the stage, and we're all part,
In this laughter-filled haven, a joy-filled heart.

Melodies Beneath the Moonlit Sky

Under moonlight, shadows start to dance,
A flamingo prances, what a funny chance!
The gentle waves, they giggle and sigh,
As they whisper secrets to the night sky.

Coconuts roll, giggles in the breeze,
Turtles wear hats, now that's a tease!
A crab does the cha-cha on the sand,
While the stars wink down, playful and grand.

The breezes hum tunes of silly delight,
As bonfires flicker, creating warm light.
With marshmallows roasting, and laughter galore,
The night's full of joy, who could ask for more?

In a world of dreams under starlit beams,
Every creature joins in, bursting at the seams.
With music and laughter, all worries take flight,
In this moonlit wonder, everything feels right.

Driftwood Dreams and Starry Nights

On driftwood logs, we gather around,
With creatures from sea, laughter's the sound!
A dolphin cracks jokes, splashes with glee,
While seagulls squawk tales from the sea.

The stars above twinkle, each one a light,
Creating a canvas that's pure delight.
A crab on a shell plays an old guitar,
Singing silly ballads, my shining star.

The night hums along with a wobbly beat,
As sandcastles wiggle beneath our feet.
Mermaids giggle at the sight on the shore,
Inviting all dreamers to dance and explore.

Under the waves, and above in the air,
Every critter joins in, spreading good cheer.
In driftwood dreams where laughter takes flight,
With whimsy and wonder, we bask in the night.

Secrets of a Sun-Kissed Isle

On a sun-kissed isle, where the coconuts sway,
The crabs wear sunglasses, enjoying the day.
A parrot tells stories, full of great zest,
While the clams in the sand just chuckle and rest.

Every wave brings a giggle, a splash, and a cheer,
As dolphins jump high, their laughter we hear.
A turtle in flip-flops slowly parades,
While the iguanas break out in charades.

The sun sets down, painting skies red and pink,
As fireflies gather, each one winks and blinks.
"We're here to dance!" chirp the bugs of the night,
In a grove of delight, everything feels right.

In this sun-kissed isle, where joy is the key,
Every creature's a friend, come and join me!
Through laughter and song, let's dance till we drop,
In this paradise of smiles, we'll never stop!

Twilight's Gentle Grasp

As the sun says goodbye, birds begin to dance,
Crickets chirp a tune, inviting us to prance.
Cocktails in our hands, with umbrellas on top,
We twirl and we swirl, never wanting to stop.

Night falls like a blanket, wrapped snug and tight,
Raccoons steal our snacks, under the pale moonlight.
Palm trees giggle softly, swaying side to side,
While sand slips through our toes, like a funny tide.

The stars above wink down, a mischievous crew,
Jellyfish are discoing, a slippery view.
Laughter rolls like waves, crashing on the shore,
As we chase the tiny crabs, yelling, "Give us more!"

In this soft embrace, our worries take a flight,
With dreams that are as strange, as a banana in flight.
Drifting into sleep, with a smile on my face,
Tomorrow will bring more fun, and silly, wild grace.

Interlude of Ocean Whispers

Seashells hum a tune, while the palm fronds sway,
Fishes play hide-and-seek, in a funny way.
Waves that giggle softly, tickling our toes,
A crab wearing sunglasses strikes a pose.

The coconut's a hat, on a volleyball's face,
High-fives from the seagulls, what a silly race!
Beneath the bright sun, we imitate a dolphin,
Falling on the sand, it's a laughing, wild win!

Turtles roll their eyes at our attempts to swim,
While starfish cheer from rocks, laughing on a whim.
The ocean pours its secrets, with bubbles of joy,
To be a child again, is the ultimate ploy.

So let the rhythm surge, like a giggling tide,
In this whimsical world, where fun cannot hide.
With each splash and each laugh, our spirits soar high,
In a beachy, goofy thrall, beneath a sunny sky.

The Echoes of Paradise

In the shade of a palm, with chocolate in hand,
The monkeys plot mischief, oh, isn't it grand?
Fruit flies dance around, with a rhythmic delight,
While we share our snacks, in the fading light.

A pineapple's a crown, on a king of the sea,
With the ocean's soft whispers, like a symphony.
Bubble-blowing dolphins twist in playful ranks,
And we laugh at the sight, giving playful pranks.

The sand shimmies and shakes, as footsteps abound,
While lizards join our jest, with a flick and a bound.
Sunset paints the skies in pastel hues of fun,
The laughter of the coast, an everlasting run.

Pirates of the waves shout, "Join our crew today!"
With treasures of pure joy, come out and play.
As the breezy night whispers tales oh so sweet,
We fall for the charm, in this funny retreat.

Laughter Amongst the Stars

When the moon's on a swing, and the stars laugh bright,
We play hopscotch with shadows, in the soft twilight.
A pelican tells jokes, with a beak wide and bold,
While jellybeans rain down, a treasure of gold.

Gravity takes a break, as we float in the air,
Rafting on dreams, without a single care.
Lizards with sunglasses, strut down the path,
While we burst into giggles, in this midnight bath.

Octopi juggle shells, with their eight funny arms,
Trying to impress, with their underwater charms.
The beach is a canvas, for our laughter's art,
Creating waves of joy, that dance in the dark.

As we sway with the breeze, under a starlit sky,
The night wraps us snug, like a blanket nearby.
In this whirl of delight, where the cosmic gigs start,
We cradle our dreams, as we laugh from the heart.

A Voyage in Softness

On a boat made of pillows, we sail so high,
Chasing giggling seagulls that dance in the sky.
With marshmallow waves that tickle our toes,
And jellybean sunbeams that fizz and glow.

Pirates of laughter, we sip coconut milk,
As the clouds turn to candy, soft as silk.
We plunder our snacks, we giggle and cheer,
This sweet little voyage brings us nothing but cheer.

A parrot in shades squawks tunes that he knows,
While a dolphin does flips, in his sparkly clothes.
With each splash of joy, our hearts take a flight,
Tomorrow brings more, and oh, what delight!

Together we giggle, with stars as our guide,
In a sailboat of softness, we joyously glide.
For every small wave is a giggle unfurled,
In this fluffy adventure, we conquer the world!

Love's Gentle Breeze

A breeze like a whisper, so sweet and so sly,
Blows kisses on faces, as we laugh and fly.
Tropical fruits giggle in baskets so bright,
While butterflies twirl in a dance of pure light.

In this sunny garden, where giggles are spun,
We play hide and seek, oh, what endless fun!
The flowers, they tease with their colorful clothes,
Dancing together, the love in us grows.

A picnic of laughter, with lemonade streams,
We nibble on cookies, and flow like our dreams.
With every soft touch, joy softly unfolds,
Love's gentle breeze, the secret life holds.

So let's sway with the trees, in rainbows of cheer,
With giggles aplenty, and friends ever near.
Each moment a treasure, in laughter we blend,
In this place of delight, where the fun won't end.

Lullaby of Shimmering Sands

The beach sings a tune, with grains of pure gold,
Shells play the maracas, with stories retold.
A crab in a conch plays a rhythm so bright,
While sandcastles giggle in the shimmering light.

Each wave is a song, soft whispers of play,
As flip-flops tap dance, come join in the sway.
The sun wears a smile that's as wide as the sea,
While ice cream is melting, oh what glee!

Seagulls are jesters, with jokes up their wings,
A treasure chest brimming with joyous spring things.
With laughter like bubbles, we drift in the flow,
Sand tickles our toes, as we dance to and fro.

At night, stars play peekaboo, giggling so bright,
As we whisper our dreams to the soft moonlight.
Together we sigh, with the beach all aglow,
In this lullaby sweet, where laughter will grow.

Moonbeams and Monsoons

Clouds wearing pajamas come drifting by slow,
While raindrops are giggling, putting on a show.
Moonbeams are winking, they dance on the tide,
In a puddle of laughter where secrets reside.

The frogs croak a chorus, a comical band,
While we wear our boots, splashing joy on the land.
With each tiny river, our hearts come alive,
In this rainy fiesta, together we thrive.

The trees join the dance, in a twirly parade,
As we spin in a circle, unafraid, unmade.
With laughter like thunder, we leap and we play,
In this silly downpour, we'll never betray.

So let's revel in moonbeams, in monsoons we trust,
For joy's endless rhythm turns laughter to dust.
With every soft patter, our worries dissolve,
In this goofy wet world, we're free to evolve!

Whispers of the Coconut Breeze

Beneath the swaying trees so wide,
Coconuts giggle as they collide.
Monkeys throw jokes, oh what a spree,
While flamingos dance with glee.

The parrot squawks a cheeky rhyme,
Time for a nap? Oh, never mind!
The sun's too bright for sleepyheads,
Let's chase our shadows instead!

Sandy toes in bright green sea,
Jellyfish wiggle, wild and free.
A crab attempts a funny walk,
While starfish share their silly talk.

So let the waves tickle your feet,
With every splash, there's laughter sweet.
The breeze whispers jokes in the night,
As we drift off, all feels right.

Serenity Under Palm Fronds

Beneath the palms, a secret place,
Where sea turtles glide with grace.
A squirrel drops a nut in fun,
As dolphins leap, they're on the run.

Laughter echoes in the bay,
As crabs navigate their tricky way.
A hermit crab tries on a shoe,
'Oh, this won't do!' he says, 'Just two!"

Sunset paints the sky in cheer,
As fireflies start to appear.
A gecko sings a silly tune,
And joins the party under the moon.

So close your eyes, just breathe it in,
The joy of life where laughter's been.
With whispers soft and spirits light,
Let dreams of fun carry you tonight.

Last Light Over Coral Reefs

The coral reef sparkles with delight,
As fish parade in colors bright.
A clown fish tells a corny joke,
While seaweed starts to softly poke.

Octopuses juggle shells with flair,
One slips and lands in quite a scare!
Seahorses dance in twirling lines,
As starfish laugh at silly signs.

The day slips slowly into night,
While waves hum soft, a lullaby light.
The sunset grins with hues so bold,
As tales of silliness unfold.

Let's count the stars, oh what a sight,
And giggle softly with delight.
In waters warm, let laughter flow,
As sleepy dreams begin to grow.

Songs of the Sapphire Shores

The sapphire shores are full of fun,
Where crickets chirp until they're done.
A pelican tries to catch a fish,
But ends up with a splashing wish!

The beach ball bounces, with a squeak,
While seagulls shout, it's time to peak.
A turtle races 'round the sand,
While a wiggly worm does a handstand.

As night rolls in, the lanterns glow,
And creatures peek out, putting on a show.
A conch shell hums a cheeky song,
Inviting all to join along.

So pull up a seat, let giggles ring,
As the ocean waves begin to sing.
In this paradise, our hearts will play,
With silly sounds to light our way.

Conch Shell Echoes

A conch shell sings a silly song,
To crabs and fish that dance along.
With every blow, a bubble pops,
While seagulls mimic the funny flops.

Underneath the sunlit sky,
A parrot squawks as it flutters by.
With coconut hats and grass-skirt dreams,
The ocean giggles in sunlit beams.

The shore's a stage for antics grand,
Flip-flops flying from beachgoers' hand.
Shells compete in a clamor of noise,
While starfish join in for the poise.

A hammock sways with a gentle bounce,
As sleepyheads begin to pounce.
Waves chuckle softly like old friends,
In this seaside joy that never ends.

Breezy Banana Leaf Lullabies

A banana leaf whispers to the breeze,
Telling tales of monkeys with ease.
They swing on branches with silly grins,
While the rustling leaves burst into spins.

Coconuts roll, as if to race,
Bumping each other in a comic chase.
With every tickle from the wind's hand,
The laughter carries across the sand.

Jellyfish wear their jelly shoes,
Waltzing under skies of sunny blues.
They trip and fall, how they amuse,
As children giggle with hearty views.

The night sky calls, with twinkling stars,
While crickets chirp their funny bars.
In a hammock stitched with dreams so bright,
Laughter drifts softly into the night.

Tides and Teardrops

When tides roll in with a playful swoosh,
The sands do a dance, a wiggly woosh.
Teardrops of laughter hit the shore,
Making sea turtles beg for more.

A jellyfish juggles in the foam,
Confusing dolphins who wander home.
With every splish and every splash,
The ocean's humor makes a dash.

Seagulls squawk, bringing comic relief,
As they steal snacks, causing disbelief.
The sunset paints a colorful scene,
While waves tickle with a gentle sheen.

The stars now twinkle, giggles to share,
As crabs perform their tap dance flair.
Night's curtain falls on a playful stage,
Where tides of joy and laughter engage.

Midnight Mangrove Melodies

Beneath the moon, where shadows play,
The mangroves sway in a funny way.
With wiggly roots and singing leaves,
They hold secrets that everyone believes.

A raccoon prances on crooked land,
Holding an acorn like a grand stand.
With each little stumble, a giggle escapes,
In this merry land of fluffy shapes.

Frogs on lily pads croak out tune,
In a froggy choir under the moon.
Their quirky hops keep the rhythm sweet,
While fireflies join in, dancing on feet.

As night deepens, laughter fills air,
Critters conspire with whimsical flair.
In the mangroves, magic does swell,
With memories made, no need to dwell.

Twilight Tales from the Surf

The crabs are plotting by the shore,
With shells and whispers, they adore.
A wave comes in, they scramble away,
In flip-flops, humans join the play.

The gulls wear hats, all askew,
As sandcastles melt, it's quite the view.
A beach ball bounces off a sunburned knee,
"Oh, where's my drink?" shouts a man with glee.

The sun dips low, the sky turns pink,
As seagulls dive for your last shrimp drink.
With laughter echoing through the air,
The ocean sings; can you hear its flare?

Bring on the night, with stars in a dance,
As funny tales twist in a salty glance.
So grab your friends, and don't be shy,
In twilight tales, we'll laugh till we cry.

Breeze-Kissed Memories of Paradise

The hammock sways with a belly flop,
While coconuts cheer, "Don't you dare stop!"
A piña colada spills on a toe,
As friends strike poses for the show.

Bananas peel-off like a prank,
While palm trees giggle at the prankster's rank.
A parrot mimics with a cheeky squawk,
As the sun sets down, it's time for a walk.

The breeze whispers tales of last night's feast,
With leftover croutons devoured by a beast.
But no one complains, just shares a grin,
As laughter takes flight like a dive-bombing fin.

So raise your glasses to days gone by,
With silly moments that never say die.
In this whimsical world of sun and sand,
We'll treasure the funny, hand in hand.

Serenade of the Firefly Dance

In the dark, fireflies flash like stars,
They twirl and dip, making jokes from afar.
One of them lands on a silly hat,
Creating a glow with a little chat.

A raccoon laughs with a coconut grin,
As the moonlight glimmers, where to begin?
Each flicker whispers funny little tales,
Of clumsy fish trying to ride on gales.

The crickets join in with a swing and tap,
A symphony builds, is it nature's clap?
While owls roll their eyes and hoot with flair,
"Why do we dance? Isn't it rare?"

So sway with the shadows, let your heart prance,
In the serenade that makes shadows dance.
Underneath the stars, it's all in good fun,
As we giggle together 'til the night is done.

Night Jasmine's Sweet Release

The jasmine blooms with a scent of glee,
As night critters gather for their jubilee.
A lizard struts with a big bold flair,
"Look at me shine!" like he just doesn't care.

The moon winks down at the shimmery pool,
Where turtles groove; they make breaking cool.
A butterfly flutters, then lands on a bear,
"Excuse me, sir, have you tried my hair?"

The stars giggle softly, sharing their tricks,
As crabs tap dance, showing off slick kicks.
"Come join the fun, no need for a fence,
In this garden of giggles, life makes sense."

As the night deepens, the laughter won't cease,
With jasmine's embrace, we find sweet release.
For in every chuckle, the magic we find,
Is a blissful reminder, we leave worries behind.

The Dance of Nightfall

As the sun dips low, the crickets cry,
Dancing shadows twirl, oh me, oh my!
Fireflies flicker, a wiggly parade,
Nighttime giggles in the twilight fade.

A squirrel on a branch, doing a jig,
Twirling and swaying, oh look at him wig!
The stars burst out, like popcorn in flight,
While moonbeams chuckle, spreading delight.

The breeze whispers secrets, silly and neat,
A ticklish tickle wraps around your feet.
Laughter echoes through the leafy lanes,
As the night's dance beckons and entertains.

With a crescent smile, the night winks wide,
Join in the fun, come for the ride!
Under the blanket of the vast dark sea,
Let the laughter flow, so wild and free.

Cocoa Dreams

In the forest thick, a chocolate stream,
Rabbits sip cocoa, living the dream.
Marshmallow clouds float above their heads,
Laughing and bouncing from their soft beds.

A monkey in shades jokes with a bear,
Who snorts chocolate milk, fluffs up his hair.
Balloons of fudge float up in the sky,
Giggling aloud, they dance as they fly.

Beneath the cocoa trees, sweet smells arise,
Where funny creatures wear syrupy ties.
Whisking up giggles, stirring delight,
In a world made of sweet, everything feels right.

So come join the fun, just follow your nose,
Where laughter is plenty and joy freely flows.
In this dreamland of cocoa, let's take a leap,
And drift on the waves of a sugary sleep.

Moonlit Canopy

Under a canopy of glimmering light,
The owls spin tales of the silliest sight.
Raccoons in tuxedos are ready to glide,
On a slip-and-slide, watch their joy collide!

Lemurs wear hats, with feathers so bright,
Juggling and tumbling, oh what a sight!
Coconut drums beat as they prance and sway,
With giggles and grins, they steal the display.

A breeze plays the harp, with strings made of mist,
While critters join in, none dare to resist.
The moon grins wide, in its glowing embrace,
Cheering for friends, in this moonlit space.

So twirl with the trees, let your heart fly free,
In a canopy circus, just you and me.
Together we'll laugh, sing a silly tune,
Under the watch of the chuckling moon.

Serenade of the Seas

The fish in the sea, they tango and spin,
Wearing tiny hats, with a cheeky grin.
Octopuses flaunt eight-legged flair,
Holding a concert in the salty air.

The waves act silly, with splashes that tease,
Making the dolphins giggle with ease.
Seagulls conduct with a squawk and a flap,
Leading the symphony, a merry mishap!

Starfish with maracas shake to the beat,
While crabs in their shells tap their little feet.
A serenade rises from coral so bright,
As laughter and music light up the night.

So come dive in deep, join this whimsical spree,
Where the ocean's a stage, and we're wild and free.
In the magical waves, let's sing along,
To the serenade of the seas, where we belong.

In the Shadow of the Banyan Tree

Beneath the leaves, a monkey swings,
Chasing dreams and shiny things.
A parrot squawks a silly tune,
As geckos dance beneath the moon.

A lizard laughs, then slips away,
While crickets join in on the play.
The breeze brings scents of fruity snacks,
As laughter fills the jungle tracks.

In this green realm of clumsy cheer,
Frogs croak rhymes we wish to hear.
The banyan tree, a shelter grand,
Hosts a circus, nature's band.

With every rustle, giggles rise,
A symphony of cheerful cries.
So come and join this playful glee,
In shadows cast by a great banyan tree.

Beyond the Horizon: A Farewell Song

As boats set sail, the gulls take flight,
A captain waves with sheer delight.
The ocean's laugh, a playful tease,
With fish that dance and tickle knees.

A wave approaches, big and round,
It yanks the hat right off the ground.
With bubbles popping all around,
The sea's a clown, it makes no sound.

Goodbyes are tricky, like a game,
The sunset blushes, just the same.
With every splash, a memory sprayed,
As laughter echoes, dreams displayed.

So off we sail, with smiles wide,
Beyond the waves, let giggles ride.
In every swell, a story born,
A jolly farewell to the morn.

The Gentle Canvas of Nightfall

As stars emerge, a canvas sprawls,
The moon hangs high, a giant ball.
Fireflies dance with tiny light,
Painting giggles in the night.

A crickets' choir, off-key delight,
Rings out like jokes beneath the night.
The shadows tease, they swirl and leap,
While sleepyheads begin to creep.

A coconut falls with a loud thud,
While owls hoot tales of misfit buds.
The breeze plays pranks, a playful act,
In nature's dream, nothing's exact.

As night unfolds with stories bright,
We lay beneath the twinkling light.
In every rustle, laughter's spry,
The gentle canvas makes us sigh.

Reflections of a Seafarer's Heart

A sailor's boat sways left and right,
His parrot squawks with pure delight.
The compass spins, it goes awry,
As seagulls ask, "What's your next try?"

With every wave, the stories grow,
Of mermaids lost and fish that glow.
A treasure chest of giggles stacks,
With every splash, we're on the tracks.

The sea, a comedian, wild and free,
Tells tall tales under the banyan tree.
A wave says, "Come and take a chance!"
As dolphins join in for a dance.

So hoist the sails, let laughter steer,
In a sailor's heart, there's never fear.
With every gust, let joy embark,
On waters bright, where dreams leave a mark.

Enchanted Island Nocturne

Under the moon, coconuts sway,
A parrot sings, in a comical way.
Crabs do the cha-cha on the warm sand,
While sea turtles dance, oh isn't it grand?

Stars flicker like fireflies, so bright,
Fish chase their tails, what a silly sight.
A monkey swings by, with a grin on his face,
Claiming this island is his favorite place.

The breeze carries laughter, oh what a thrill,
As waves tickle toes, they dance on the hill.
An iguana spins tales, with glee in his tone,
Of pirates who lost their beloved scone.

So here we will laugh till the morning light,
On this enchanted isle, everything feels right.
With every breeze, we can't help but laugh,
Under stars that write our own silly path.

Captured in Ocean's Caress

The ocean's embrace feels like a warm hug,
Where sun-kissed creatures dance, oh so snug.
Crabs twirl their claws like tiny top hats,
While dolphins flip, with giggles and spats.

Seashells whistle tunes that make us grin,
A sea horse struts, while a clam wears a pin.
Jellyfish glide, in costumes so bright,
Spreading laughter under the stars at night.

A fish with a mustache swims by so fast,
With a wink and a nod, he's a comic blast.
Octopuses juggle, oh what a strange sight,
As we roll with laughter, hearts feeling light.

The ocean's caress, it tickles our toes,
As we dance with the waves, our joy only grows.
In this whimsical world, we'll always play,
Captured by laughter, come what may.

Where the Night Blooms

In corners of dusk, where giggles brew,
Blooming at night, in a carnival hue.
Fireflies sparkle like tiny disco balls,
As sleepy palm trees wear party shawls.

A raccoon with shades does a moonwalk dance,
Frogs join in chorus, they sing with a prance.
The scent of sweet flowers drifts overhead,
While sleepy iguanas dream in their bed.

Stars wink at the night, like they're in on the joke,
As a turtle in flip-flops gives laughter a poke.
Breezes whisper secrets in the shade,
While the laughter of night serenades.

Here where the night blooms, we'll chuckle and cheer,
With a joke on our lips and lots of good cheer.
In this garden of giggles, we'll sing till we swoon,
Under sparkly skies, playing night's happy tune.

To the Rhythm of the Surf

Waves crash like drums, in a playful beat,
As sea otters groove, to the fun and the heat.
A sandy dance floor, where flip-flops collide,
With shells as our maracas, who can't hide?

A blue fish carts by, in sunglasses so grand,
Teaching sea snails to do the conga stand.
Starfish beginners are eager to learn,
To the rhythm of surf, they wiggle and turn.

The ocean sings sweetly, a melody fine,
With pelicans swooping, in perfect align.
In the warmth of the night, with no cares at all,
We'll sway to the surf, and have ourselves a ball.

So come take a chance, let joy be your guide,
In this world of laughter, let go and abide.
To the rhythm of surf, we'll dance 'til we tire,
In this silly paradise, we'll dance and inspire.

Hummingbird's Evening Grace

In the garden, colors collide,
Hummingbirds dance with joyful pride.
Buzzing softly, they flit and fly,
Chasing sunbeams as they sigh.

With nectar sweet, they laugh and play,
In their tiny world, it's a grand ballet.
A flower's giggle, a leaf's surprise,
As they twirl under the vast skies.

Evening falls, a gentle hum,
And the stars come out, one by one.
Hummingbirds rest, their racing fleet,
Dream of flowers, oh so sweet.

With a wink and a flutter, they're snoring now,
In their cozy nests, oh what a wow!
Nighttime wraps them, snug and tight,
Hummingbirds chuckle at dreams so bright.

Moonlight Reflections on Still Waters

Under the moon, the water's a tease,
Rippling laughter carried by the breeze.
Frogs in tuxedos croak their delight,
Synchronized swimming in the pale moonlight.

A fish jumps up with a splashy cheer,
Says to the moon, "Look, I'm a deer!"
Crickets join in with their own odd tune,
While shadows waltz under the watchful moon.

The stars giggle, forming a band,
As fish in the waters drift, take a stand.
Ripples echo with nightly glee,
Moonlit dreams, oh what a spree!

Softly they whisper, secrets to share,
In the dance of the night, there's laughter in air.
Moonlight glimmers, a silver show,
Reflections of joy, oh how they glow.

Mysteries of the Swaying Mangroves

In the mangroves, secrets abound,
Where crabs in pajamas dance all around.
Whispers of leaves, a playful tease,
As the wind giggles through branches with ease.

Pelicans pondering life from above,
Dropping fishy jokes, it's quite the love!
The mudskippers leap with a comical flair,
Wiggling their tails, oh what a pair!

Coconuts chuckle when they hit the ground,
Making the earth shake, a humorous sound.
Tides come and go, with playful intent,
A splash and a giggle, the show's never spent.

At dusk, the creatures all settle down,
In a quirky parade, no need for a crown.
Under starlit skies, they dream with delight,
In their playful world, everything feels right.

Softness of the Island Slumber

On the island, the palms sway and hum,
Lullabies of coconuts, sweet and dumb.
Sand tickles toes, a gentle embrace,
As crabs in pajamas scuttle with grace.

The sea whispers tales, full of jest,
As shells share secrets from their cozy nest.
The horizon yawns, in shades of gold,
Dreams of adventure, so bold and untold.

A gentle breeze cradles the night,
While owls wear glasses, wise and bright.
Stars giggle softly, twinkling away,
As the island catches dreams in its sway.

Whether napping or playing, the island declares,
A unique bedtime story, free of cares.
With each splash of waves, they sigh and twine,
A world painted bright, with laughter divine.

www.ingramcontent.com/pod-product-compliance
Lightning Source LLC
Chambersburg PA
CBHW072218070526
44585CB00015B/1397